SWAMI VIVEKANANDA SLOGANS

SWAMI VIVEKANANDA SLOGANS

S.KRISHNA SAI TEJA

1:"Take risks in your life, If you win, you can lead! If you loose, you can guide!

2: "Strength is life; weakness is death."

3: "Experience is the only teacher we have. we may talk and reason all our lives, but we shall not understand a word of truth."

4: "If you think yourselves strong, strong you will be."

5: "Take up one idea, make that one idea your life. Think of it, dream of it, Live on that idea let the brain, muscles, nerves, every part of your body be full of that idea, and just leave every other idea alone. This is the way to success."

6: "Stand up, be bold, and take the blame on your own shoulders. Do not go about throwing mud at other; for all the faults you suffer from, you are the sole and only cause."

7: "Meditation can turn fools in to sages but unfortunately fools never meditate."

8: "Learn everything that is good from others, but bring it in, and in your own way adsorb it; do not become others."

9: "In a conflict between the heart and the brain, follow your heart."

Advertisement

10: "That man has reached immortality who is disturbed by nothing material."

Advertisement

Contents

Foreword

11: "You should work like a master and not as a slave; work incessantly, but do not do a slave's work."

12: "Whatever you believe, that you will be, If you believe yourselves to be ages, ages you will be tomorrow. There is nothing to obstruct you."

13: "If i love myself despite my infinite faults, how can i hate anyone at the glimpse of a few faults"..!

14: "You cannot believe in god until you believe in yourself."

15: "All power is within you. You can do anything and everything. Believe in that. Do not believe that you are weak; do not believe that you are half-crazy lunatics, as most of us do nowadays. Stand up and express the divinity within you."

16: "You are the creator of your own destiny."

17: "That which is selfish is immoral, and that which is unselfish is moral."

Advertisement

18: "Talk to yourself once in a day.. otherwise you may miss meeting an excellent person in this world."

19: "Throw away all weakness. tell your body that it is strong. Tell your mind that it is strong and have unbound faith and hope in yourself."

20: "All power is within you; you can do anything and everything."

Preface

21: "When you are doing any work.. do it as worship, as he highest worship, and devote your whole life to it for the time being."

22: "The mistake is that we want to tie the whole world down to our own plane of thought and to make out mind the measure of the whole universe."

23: "We are what our thought have made us; So take care about what you think. Words are secondary. Thoughts live; They travel far."

24: "Have faith in yourself – all power is in you. Even the poison of a snake is powerless, if you can firmly deny it."

25: "You have to grow from the inside out. None can teach you, none can make you spiritual. There is no other teacher but your own soul."

26: "Have faith in yourselves, great convictions are the mothers of great deeds."

27: "If superstitions enters, the brain is gone"

28: "The world is the great gymnasium where we come to make ourselves strong."

29: Best Vivekananda quotes with images.

30: Vivekananda quotes about success with pictures.

Acknowledgements

31: "Arise awake and stop not until the goal is achieved."

32: "Dare to be free dare to go as far as you're thought leads, and dare to carry that out in your life."

33: "The fire that warms us can also consume us; it is not the fault of the fire."

34: "Arise awake – All the powers in the universe are already ours. It is we who have put our hands before our eyes and cry that it is dark."

35: " We are what our thoughts have made us; so take care about what you think."

36: "Do not hate anybody, because that hatred which comes out from you must, in the long run, come back to you, if you love, that love will come back to you, completing the circle."

37: "Both attachment and detachment perfectly developed make a man great and happy."

38: "Where can we go to find GOD if we cannot see him in ours own hearts and in every living being."

39: "This life is short, the vanities of the world are transient, but they alone live who live for others, the rest are more dead than alive."

40: "The calmer we are and the less disturbed our nerves, the more shall we love ad the better will our work."

Prologue

41: "The power of concentration is the only key to the treasure-house of knowledge."

42: "If you really my children, you will fear nothing, stop at nothing, you will be like lions,,, My prayers and benedictions follow every step you take… everything will come to you if you have faith."

43: "Neither money pays, not name, nor fame, nor learning; it is CHARACTER that an cleave through adamantine walls of difficulties."

44: "Each work has to pass through these stages – ridicule, opposition, and then acceptance. Those who think ahead of their time are sure to be misunderstood."

45: "Conquer yourself and the whole universe is yours."

46: "3 Golden rules!! Who is helping you, don't forget them. Who is loving you, don't hate them. Who is trusting you, don't cheat them."

47: "Don't look back -forward infinite energy, infinite enthusiasm, infinite daring, and infinite patience – then alone can great deeds be accomplished."

48: "I am proud to belong to a religion which has taught the world tolerance & universal acceptance. we believe not only in universal toleration but we accept all religion as true."

49: "Never think there is anything impossible for the soul."

50: "The greatest sin is to think that you are weak."

Slogans

1. "Do not wait for anybody or anything. Do whatever you can, build your hope on none."

-Swami Vivekananda.

2. "The best thermometer to the progress of a nation is its treatment of its women."

-Swami Vivekananda.

3. "Experience is the only teacher we have. We may talk and reason all our lives, but we shall not understand a word of truth."

-Swami Vivekananda.

4. "Take risks in your life. If you win, you can lead, if you lose, you can guide."

-Swami Vivekananda.

5. "Golden rules: Who is helping you, don't forget them. Who is loving you, don't hate them. Who is trusting you, don't cheat them."

-Swami Vivekananda.

6. "When I asked God for strength, he gave me difficult situations to face."

-Swami Vivekananda.

7. "The reason for every misunderstanding is that we see the people as we are but not as they are."

-Swami Vivekananda.

8. "Every act of love brings happiness; there is no act of love which does not bring peace and blessedness as its reaction."

-Swami Vivekananda.

9. "All differences in this world are of degree, and not of kind, because oneness is the secret of everything."

-Swami Vivekananda.

10. "See for the highest, aim at the highest, and you shall reach the highest."

-Swami Vivekananda.

Slogans

11. "The fire that warms us can also consume us; it is not the fault of the fire."

-Swami Vivekananda.

12. "God helps those who help themselves."

-Swami Vivekananda.

13. "He who struggles is better than he who never attempts."

-Swami Vivekananda.

14. "Let men have light, let them be pure and spiritually strong and educated, then alone will misery cease in the world, not before."

-Swami Vivekananda.

15. "When an idea exclusively occupies the mind, it is transformed into an actual physical or mental state."

-Swami Vivekananda.

16. "The greatest religion is to be true to your nature. Have faith in yourselves."

-Swami Vivekananda.

17. "When a man is under the control of senses. He is of the world. When he has controlled the senses the world is of him."

-Swami Vivekananda.

18. "Death is but a change."

-Swami Vivekananda.

19. "A man is not poor without a rupee but a man is really poor without a dream and ambition."

-Swami Vivekananda.

20. "External nature is only internal nature writ large."

Slogans

21. "We are what our thoughts have made us; so take care about what you think. Words are secondary. Thoughts live; they travel far."

-Swami Vivekananda.

22. "In a conflict between the heart and the brain, follow your heart."

-Swami Vivekananda.

23. "Arise! Awake! and stop not until the goal is reached."

-Swami Vivekananda.

24. "Do one thing at a time, and while doing it put your whole soul into it to the exclusion of all else."

-Swami Vivekananda.

25. "You have to grow from the inside out. None can teach you, none can make you spiritual. There is no other teacher but your own soul."

-Swami Vivekananda.

26. "Anything that makes weak - physically, intellectually and spiritually, reject it as poison."

-Swami Vivekananda.

27. "Take up one idea, make that one idea your life, think of it, dream of it, live on that idea. Let the brain, muscles, nerves, every part of your body be full of that idea, and just leave every other idea alone. This is the way to success."

-Swami Vivekananda.

28. "Purity, patience, and perseverance are the three essentials to success and above all, love."

-Swami Vivekananda.

29. "That man has reached immortality who is disturbed by nothing material."

-Swami Vivekananda.

30. "The world is the great gymnasium where we come to make ourselves strong."

-Swami Vivekananda.

Slogans

31. "True progress is slow but sure."

-Swami Vivekananda.

32. "The gift of knowledge is the highest gift in the world."

-Swami Vivekananda.

33. "The brain and muscles must develop simultaneously. Iron nerves with an intelligent brain — and the whole world is at your feet."

-Swami Vivekananda.

34. "Had I lived in Palestine, in the days of Jesus of Nazareth, I would have washed his feet, not with my tears, but with my heart's blood!"

-Swami Vivekananda.

35. "God is to be worshipped as the one beloved, dearer than everything in this and next life."

-Swami Vivekananda.

36. "Christ, being man, had to see impurity and denounced it; but God, infinitely higher, does not see iniquity and cannot be angry."

-Swami Vivekananda.

37. "The more we come out and do good to others, the more our hearts will be purified, and God will be in them"

- Swami Vivekananda.

38. "Father is the existence out of which everything comes; Son is that knowledge. It is in Christ that God will be manifest. God was everywhere, in all beings, before Christ; but in Christ we became conscious of Him."

-Swami Vivekananda.

39. "I pity the Hindu who does not see the beauty in Jesus Christ's character. I pity the Christian who does not reverence the Hindu Christ."

-Swami Vivekananda.

40. "You cannot believe in God until you believe in yourself."
-Swami Vivekananda.

Slogans

40. "You cannot believe in God until you believe in yourself."

-Swami Vivekananda.

41. "Everything is easy when you are busy. But nothing is easy when you are lazy."

-Swami Vivekananda.

42. "Where can we go to find God if we cannot see Him in our own hearts and in every living being."

-Swami Vivekananda.

43. "God is here in all these human souls."

-Swami Vivekananda.

44. "Learn everything that is good from others, but bring it in, and in your own way absorb it; do not become others."

-Swami Vivekananda.

45. "So long as there is desire or want, it is a sure sign that there is imperfection. A perfect, free being cannot have any desire."

-Swami Vivekananda.

46. "All the powers in the universe are already ours. It is we who have put our hands before our eyes and cry that it is dark."

-Swami Vivekananda.

47. "In one word, this ideal is that you are divine."

-Swami Vivekananda.

48. "Be true unto death."

-Swami Vivekananda.

49. "The powers of the mind are like the rays of the sun dissipated. When they are concentrated, they illumine."

-Swami Vivekananda.

50. "Comfort is no test of truth. Truth is often far from being comfortable."

-Swami Vivekananda.

Slogans

SLOGANS51. "Talk to yourself once in a day, otherwise you may miss meeting an intelligent person in this world."

-Swami Vivekananda.

52. "If I love myself despite my infinite faults, how can I hate anyone at the glimpse of a few faults."

-Swami Vivekananda.

53. "Do not lower your goals to the level of your abilities. Instead, raise your abilities to the height of your goals."

-Swami Vivekananda.

54. "Books are infinite in number and time is short. The secret of knowledge is to take what is essential. Take that and try to live up to it."

-Swami Vivekananda.

55. "The mind is but the subtle part of the body. You must retain great strength in your mind and words."

-Swami Vivekananda.

56. "First, believe in the world—that there is meaning behind everything."

-Swami Vivekananda.

57. "Death is the result of inaction."

Swami Vivekananda Biography

Swami Vivekananda 12 January 1863 – 4 July 1902), born Narendranath Datta (Bengali: [nɔrendronatʰ dɔto]), was an Indian Hindu monk and philosopher. He was a chief disciple of the 19th-century Indian mystic Ramakrishna. Influenced by Western esotericism, he was a key figure in the introduction of the Indian darsanas (teachings, practices) of Vedanta and Yoga to the Western world,and is credited with raising interfaith awareness, bringing Hinduism to the status of a major world religion during the late 19th century. He was a major force in the contemporary Hindu reform movements in India, and contributed to the concept of nationalism in colonial India.Vivekananda founded the Ramakrishna Math and the Ramakrishna Mission. He is perhaps best known for his speech which began with the words "Sisters and brothers of America ...," in which he introduced Hinduism at the Parliament of the World's Religions in Chicago in 1893.

Born into an aristocratic Bengali Kayastha family of Calcutta, Vivekananda was inclined towards spirituality. He was influenced by his guru, Ramakrishna, from whom he learnt that all living beings were an embodiment of the divine self; therefore, service to God could be rendered by service to humankind. After Ramakrishna's death, Vivekananda toured the Indian subcontinent extensively and acquired first-hand knowledge of the conditions prevailing in British India. He later travelled to the United States, representing India at the 1893 Parliament of the World's Religions. Vivekananda conducted hundreds of public and private lectures and classes, disseminating tenets of Hindu philosophy in the United States, England and Europe. In India, Vivekananda is regarded as a patriotic saint, and his birthday is celebrated as National Youth Day.

Swami Vivekananda Education

In 1871, at the age of eight, Narendranath enrolled at Ishwar Chandra Vidyasagar's Metropolitan Institution, where he went to school until his family moved to Raipur in 1877. In 1879, after his family's return to Calcutta, he was the only student to receive first-division marks in the Presidency College entrance examination. He was an avid reader in a wide range of subjects, including philosophy, religion, history, social science, art and literature. He was also interested in Hindu scriptures, including the Vedas, the Upanishads, the Bhagavad Gita, the Ramayana, the Mahabharata and the Puranas. Narendra was trained in Indian classical music, and regularly participated in physical exercise, sports and organised activities. Narendra studied Western logic, Western philosophy and European history at the General Assembly's Institution (now known as the Scottish Church College). In 1881, he passed the Fine Arts examination, and completed a Bachelor of Arts degree in 1884.Narendra studied the works of David Hume, Immanuel Kant, Johann Gottlieb Fichte, Baruch Spinoza, Georg W. F. Hegel, Arthur Schopenhauer, Auguste Comte, John Stuart Mill and Charles Darwin. He became fascinated with the evolutionism of Herbert Spencer and corresponded with him, translating Herbert Spencer's book Education (1861) into Bengali. While studying Western philosophers, he also learned Sanskrit scriptures and Bengali literature.

William Hastie (principal of Christian College, Calcutta, from where Narendra graduated) wrote, "Narendra is really a genius. I have travelled far and wide but I have never come across a lad of his talents and possibilities, even in German universities, among philosophical students. He is bound to make his mark in life".

Narendra was known for his prodigious memory and the ability at speed reading. Several incidents have been given as examples. In a talk, he once quoted verbatim, two or three pages from Pickwick Papers. Another incident that is given is his argument with a Swedish national where he gave reference to some details on Swedish history that the Swede originally disagreed with but later conceded. In another incident with Dr. Paul Deussen's at Kiel in Germany, Vivekananda was going over some poetical work and did not reply when the professor spoke to him. Later, he apologised to Dr. Deussen explaining that he was too absorbed in reading and hence did not hear him. The professor was not satisfied with this explanation, but Vivekananda quoted and interpreted verses from the text, leaving the professor dumbfounded about his feat of memory. Once, he requested some books written by Sir John Lubbock from a library and returned them the very next day, claiming that he had read them. The librarian refused to believe him until cross-examination about the contents convinced him that Vivekananda was being truthful.

Some accounts have called Narendra a shrutidhara (a person with a prodigious memory).

Swami Vivekananda Travils In India

In 1888, Narendra left the monastery as a Parivrâjaka— the Hindu religious life of a wandering monk, "without fixed abode, without ties, independent and strangers wherever they go". His sole possessions were a kamandalu (water pot), staff and his two favourite books: the Bhagavad Gita and The Imitation of Christ. Narendra travelled extensively in India for five years, visiting centres of learning and acquainting himself with diverse religious traditions and social patterns. He developed sympathy for the suffering and poverty of the people, and resolved to uplift the nation. Living primarily on bhiksha (alms), Narendra travelled on foot and by railway (with tickets bought by admirers). During his travels he met, and stayed with Indians from all religions and walks of life: scholars, dewans, rajas, Hindus, Muslims, Christians, paraiyars (low-caste workers) and government officials. Narendra left Bombay for Chicago on 31 May 1893 with the name "Vivekananda", as suggested by Ajit Singh of Khetri,which means "the bliss of discerning wisdom," from Sanskrit viveka and ānanda.

About Ramakrishna

In 1881 Narendra first met Ramakrishna, who became his spiritual focus after his own father had died in 1884.

Narendra's first introduction to Ramakrishna occurred in a literature class at General Assembly's Institution when he heard Professor William Hastie lecturing on William Wordsworth's poem, The Excursion. While explaining the word "trance" in the poem, Hastie suggested that his students visit Ramakrishna of Dakshineswar to understand the true meaning of trance. This prompted some of his students (including Narendra) to visit Ramakrishna.

They probably first met personally in November 1881,[note 1] though Narendra did not consider this their first meeting, and neither man mentioned this meeting later. At this time, Narendra was preparing for his upcoming F. A. examination, when Ram Chandra Datta accompanied him to Surendra Nath Mitra's, house where Ramakrishna was invited to deliver a lecture. According to Makarand Paranjape, at this meeting Ramakrishna asked young Narendra to sing. Impressed by his singing talent, he asked Narendra to come to Dakshineshwar.

In late 1881 or early 1882, Narendra went to Dakshineswar with two friends and met Ramakrishna. This meeting proved to be a turning point in his life. Although he did not initially accept Ramakrishna as his teacher and rebelled against his ideas, he was attracted by his personality and began to frequently visit him at Dakshineswar. He initially saw Ramakrishna's ecstasies and visions as "mere figments of imagination" and "hallucinations".As a member of Brahmo Samaj, he opposed idol worship, polytheism and Ramakrishna's worship of Kali. He even rejected the Advaita Vedanta of "identity with the absolute" as blasphemy and madness, and often ridiculed the idea. Narendra tested Ramakrishna, who faced his arguments patiently: "Try to see the truth from all angles", he replied.

Narendra's father's sudden death in 1884 left the family bankrupt; creditors began demanding the repayment of loans, and relatives threatened to evict the family from their ancestral home. Narendra, once a son of a well-to-do family, became one of the poorest students in his college. He unsuccessfully tried to find work and questioned God's existence, but found solace in Ramakrishna and his visits to Dakshineswar increased.

One day, Narendra requested Ramakrishna to pray to goddess Kali for their family's financial welfare. Ramakrishna suggested him to go to the temple himself and pray. Following Ramakrishna's suggestion, he went to the temple thrice, but failed to pray for any kind of worldly necessities and ultimately prayed for true knowledge and devotion from the goddess.Narendra gradually grew ready to renounce everything for the sake of realising God, and accepted Ramakrishna as his Guru.

In 1885, Ramakrishna developed throat cancer, and was transferred to Calcutta and (later) to a garden house in Cossipore. Narendra and Ramakrishna's other disciples took care of him during his last days, and Narendra's spiritual education continued. At Cossipore, he experienced Nirvikalpa samadhi. Narendra and several other disciples received ochre robes from Ramakrishna, forming his first monastic order. He was taught that service to men was the most effective worship of God. Ramakrishna asked him to care for the other monastic disciples, and in turn asked them to see Narendra as their leader.[Ramakrishna died in the early-morning hours of 16 August 1886 in Cossipore.

Swami Vivekananda Death

On 4 July 1902 (the day of his death), Vivekananda awoke early, went to the monastery at Belur Math and meditated for three hours. He taught Shukla-Yajur-Veda, Sanskrit grammar and the philosophy of yoga to pupils, later discussing with colleagues a planned Vedic college in the Ramakrishna Math. At 7:00 PM Vivekananda went to his room, asking not to be disturbed; he died at 9:20 p.m. while meditating. According to his disciples, Vivekananda attained mahasamādhi; the rupture of a blood vessel in his brain was reported as a possible cause of death. His disciples believed that the rupture was due to his brahmarandhra (an opening in the crown of his head) being pierced when he attained mahasamādhi. Vivekananda fulfilled his prophecy that he would not live forty years. He was cremated on a sandalwood funeral pyre on the bank of the Ganga in Belur, opposite where Ramakrishna was cremated sixteen years earlier.